GAYLORD R

MONEY AROUND THE WORLD

MONEY

Patricia Armentrout

The Rourke Press, Inc.
Vero Beach, Florida 32964

PHOTO CREDITS
© Corel Corporation: Cover, Title, pgs.10, 17; © East Coast
Studios: pgs. 7, 8, 15; © James P. Rowan: pg. 4; © Elwin Trump:
pg. 12; © Oscar C. Williams: pg. 13; The Smithsonian Institution
National Numismatic Collection: pg. 18, 21

ACKNOWLEDGMENTS
The author acknowledges David Armentrout for his contribution in
writing this book.

Library of Congress Cataloging-in-Publication Data

Armentrout, Patricia, 1960 -
    Money around the world / by Patricia Armentrout
       p. cm. — (Money)
    Includes index.
    Summary: Briefly describes the money used in some of the
countries around the world and how money is exchanged between
countries through trade and tourism.
    ISBN 1-57103-123-5
    1. Money—Juvenile literature. 2. Foreign exchange—Juvenile
literature. 3. Coins—Juvenile literature. [1. Foreign exchange.
2. Money.]
I. Title II. Series: Armentrout, Patricia, 1960 -   Money.
HG221.5.A696 1996
332.4—dc20
                                                      96–4564
                                                       CIP
                                                       AC

Printed in the USA

TABLE OF CONTENTS

Money Around the World   5
Foreign Currency   6
Trade Between Countries   9
United States Money   11
North of the Border   14
South of the Border   16
Scandinavian Money   19
Money From China and Japan   20
Germany, France, and Italy   22
Glossary   23
Index   24

MONEY AROUND THE WORLD

Why does money from other countries look different? Countries design money using their own written language, pictures, and symbols.

Money from other countries has different **values** (VAL yooz) too. Value means how much it is worth or how much it can buy.

Because Mexican and U. S. money has different values, 50 U. S. dollars will buy more video games than 50 Mexican pesos.

Beautiful handmade goods are often bought at local street markets

FOREIGN CURRENCY

Currency (KER en see), or money, from countries other than your own is called foreign currency.

When traveling around the world, people trade, or **exchange** (eks CHAINJ), their own country's money for the money of the country they are visiting. People exchange money because most businesses do not accept foreign money.

Exchanging your own country's money for local money can be done at a bank. Bank workers have money charts that show how much local money to give in exchange for foreign money.

Many banks display the exchange rates of money from other countries

FOREIGN CURRENCY EXCHANGE

	Country	Rate
	AUSTRALIA	·7041
	CANADA	·6938
	DENMARK	·1636
	FINLAND	·2046
	FRANCE	·1844
	GERMANY	·6401
	ITALY	·00059
	JAPAN	·00887
	MEXICO	·1213
	SPAIN	·00748
	SWEDEN	·1327
	UNITED KINGDOM	1·4558

TRADE BETWEEN COUNTRIES

When a business in one country, buys, sells, or trades goods with a business in another country, it is called foreign trade. Lumber, corn, wheat, and goods made in factories are some of the products exchanged between countries.

Goods traded between countries can be paid for with money or with other goods. Although trading goods for goods was a practice that began hundreds of years ago, when there was no money, it is still done in foreign trade today.

Ships with goods from all over the world are unloaded at this busy seaport

OF AMERICA
B11752316V
WASHINGTON, D.C.
2
1
SERIES 1988 A
THE DEPARTMENT OF THE TREASURY
1789
IN GOD WE TRUST
LIBERTY
1991

UNITED STATES MONEY

The United States money system is based on the dollar. The U. S. dollar equals 100 cents. The coins used most often are the 1-cent penny, the 5-cent nickel, the 10-cent dime, and the 25-cent quarter dollar.

All United States paper money, or bills, are made the same size. A different portrait is printed on each value, or **denomination** (de NOM uh NAY shun) of bill. Each bill is printed with the same greenish-black ink. In some countries, paper money is printed in many colors.

This U. S. one-dollar bill has the same value as 100 pennies

These German notes can be exchanged for U. S. dollars at many U. S. banks

Most Mexican vendors will accept U. S. and local currency for their sales

NORTH OF THE BORDER

Canada, the country just north of the United States, also has money based on the dollar. In Canada, paper bills are printed in 1,000-dollar, 500-dollar, 50-dollar, 20-dollar, 10-dollar, 5-dollar, 2-dollar, and 1-dollar values.

Canada trades goods and services with many countries, but its largest trading partner is the United States. Canada buys, or **imports** (IM ports), food products, chemical products, and computers from the U. S. The United States imports oil, lumber, and machinery from Canada.

Unlike the United States, Canada still issues two-dollar bills

SOUTH OF THE BORDER

Mexico's currency is based on the peso. Mexico shares the second longest border with the United States. Mexico and the U. S. also share an important trade relationship.

Mexico is the largest producer of silver in the world. Mexican businesses sell silver to the U. S., as well as other products from the earth, like oil and natural gas.

The United States sells, or **exports** (EK sports), billions of dollars worth of machinery, chemicals and factory-made goods to Mexico.

This Mexican note shows its worth as 2000 pesos

SVERIGES
RIKSBANK

50

FEMTIO KRONOR

GUSTAV III 1771-1792

1965 F
B 699803

SCANDINAVIAN MONEY

Scandinavia (SKAN de NAY vee ah) is a region of northern Europe. Currency names in some Scandinavian countries have different spellings but have the same meanings.

Money from Denmark and Norway is called krone. Money from Sweden is called krona. The names mean "crown."

Sweden was the first European country to make and issue paper money. Sweden also issued the biggest coins ever made. The coins were copper plates that weighed as much as 42 pounds!

MONEY FROM CHINA AND JAPAN

A very long time ago, traders from America and Europe took silver dollars to China and Japan. Dollars are called yuan in China and yen in Japan.

China and Japan played a big part in the development of paper money. Chinese store owners began giving paper receipts to people in exchange for their coins. Japan soon adopted the idea of paper money.

Today American, Chinese, and Japanese currencies are exchanged often due to foreign trade and **tourism** (TOOR iz im).

These 14th century coins called Florins were made in Florence, Italy

GERMANY, FRANCE, AND ITALY

Germany, France, and Italy have different money today; but old coins from these countries had common designs.

Some early coins used in France had Italian designs. Some early German silver coins had French designs. One **ancient** (AIN shent) gold coin made in two Italian cities, Florence and Venice, was used as a model for the first German gold coins.

Today German money is called the mark; French money is called the franc; and Italian money is called the lira.

Glossary

ancient (AIN shent) — very old; from times long past

currency (KER en see) — money

denomination (de NOM uh NAY shun) — a value or size in a series of related values

exchange (eks CHAINJ) — to give in return for something received; to give one currency for another

exports (EK sports) — sends or sells items to foreign countries

imports (IM ports) — receives or buys items from other countries

Scandinavia (SKAN de NAY vee ah) — a term used to describe the northernmost region of Europe

tourism (TOOR iz im) — traveling for pleasure

value (VAL yoo) — the amount of money something is worth or the fair exchange for something

INDEX

ancient   22
coin   11, 19, 20, 22
currency   6, 16, 19, 20
denomination   11
dollar   11, 14, 16, 20
export   16
foreign currency   6
franc   22
imports   14
krona   19
krone   19

lira   22
mark   22
money   5, 6, 9, 11, 14, 19, 20, 22
peso   16
Scandinavia   19
tourism   20
trade   6, 9, 14, 16, 20
value   5, 11